Slow Dance on a Whirling Chair

by

Kimbally A. Medeiros

PublishAmerica
Baltimore

First printing

ISBN: 1-60610-076-9
PUBLISHED BY PUBLISHAMERICA, LLLP
www.publishamerica.com
Baltimore

Printed in the United States of America

For Alex, my love—
who inspires me creatively and in every aspect of life.

Acknowledgements

For my parents, Sharon and Louis Medeiros, who always fostered creativity and writing in me ever since I was a small child. They are the ones who put the pen in my hand and told me to write.

For my best friend, Roseanna Bragg, who taught me to appreciate my gift of writing and always encourages me to continue on my journeys in life.

For all of my English and Creative Writing teachers, especially poet Denise Duhamel of Florida International University, who taught me the meaning of what a poem really is.

And finally, for my dear love, Alex Rodriguez, who sees in me a gift that I don't see in myself. He has been there for me in the wee hours of the night as I banged away on the keyboard, encouraging me through all of my writings.

The Young Bird

The season, dried trees and leaves—
You, an abundance of mere sorrow wrapped in cloth,
Like a man cast away in an insane asylum.
Yes, you—how you weep like the trees and leaves
Drooping
Drooping
You cannot break your grief—
For she left in such a haste
Such turmoil
Such distress
She, stricken by the bite of trouble—
She was only 19 and couldn't forget her first lover past
Yes, she—how she moved you—
To tears
With her dancing butterflies and rite of passage rituals
Yes, she—She was the one who knew how to turn your regret
Now, here you are—
Nothing can change the distress caused by the 19-year-old
But, blame is only on you
For a 34-year-old should have nothing to do with such a young
bird—
Yes, she knew nothing of her charms
And yet, you blame her
You, a vast waste of infinite mourning—
Shall raise your head again to the new day, the new season
The new season, fresh flowers and springtime glories

You, bracing yourself against the new day
Like a songbird finding a berry in the glorious morning sun
Yes, you—how you've taken control and smile like fresh flowers and springtime glories
Rising
Rising
You cannot break your joy—
For she's back, she's returned
Such happiness
Such bliss

The Road from You to Me

I took a walk down a deserted pebble road that led to you,
Another unfamiliar and quiet road—
A promise wrapped in perfectly tied red ribbons and bows—
Of open-mindedness, sensuality, and honesty.
The road you promised was canopied with lush mahogany trees
With the sunlight piercing rays through the leaves,
Leaving contrasts of shadows and light,
Reminding me of our differences, and telling me of our likeness.
It was a safe-have with you;
You were all that you said you'd be—
A chivalrous man with a knack for conversation.
You whispered above the wind breezing through the trees
And kept the laughter rolling like ocean waves crashing on the shore.
The moment we said goodbye and parted from that road
I prophesied the dead end.
The road would not be pursued or traveled further.
The clouds blocked the sun and the road was lit with darkness.
I found my way back to my deserted pebble road,
Leading back to me.

In Remembrance of Spring

Eyelids coated with blue and green hues
Capture the iris in its deepest density
Only deep in the pupil can you see light in darkness
As the sun penetrates into the depth of the eye
Where you see the scene of the season unfold

The eye searches back to the forgotten season
The season where butterflies chime and crickets flutter
Only through the eye can we see what is real
For outside the eye is unreality

Sun-kissed blossoms waver to the delight of any passerby
The day produces joyous overtures like a symphony in bloom
Music surrounds the soul as night wanes—
And the spirit of the light comes out to play

Beauty in Tortuous Waters

"Tornados and treacherous waters come
to me in my dreams when something bad is going to happen," I said to my husband
with my piercing, fearful eyes looking at him as if he should to know too

"You're not psychic. Forget it," he said as he walked out the door with his computer
bag in hand to go to work.

But, I couldn't forget that timely dream.
For, we were heading in untrustworthy waters,
with the loss of our own identities was
becoming the loss of our marital bliss

The rough waters and tornado could not subside, yet
I kept my beauty, both inner and outer, strong—
I walked through those prophetic waters, picturesque and robust,
and kept my dreams alive by staying true to myself.

America: Mad Hypocrisy

America—
Mad hypocrisy.

You claim beauty, tolerance, freedom
And all that comes out of it is
Righteousness, racism, addiction

It's a place of commercialism
Where big spenders gain
And the homeless wane

It's a land of big profit
Where farmers abusively slaughter helpless animals
Then fight for more money in their pockets

Mad.

There's no better place than America
If you like pharmaceutical companies shoving pills at you
Generously helping you to become an addict
Where their pills are more powerful than those on the street
All for a $10 co-payment

It's a place where the mentally ill are ignored
Chastised, heckled, misunderstood
Left alone in the streets
Shoved into psychiatric wards
Only to be beaten down to humiliation
All in the name of medicine

America—
Mad hypocrisy.

Dreams Are to Live

Like a sole daisy standing tall in the middle of a grass field
I stand tall in the middle of my dusty living room
Life has not given me many choices but
I succumb to each challenge like they are
Adventures that need to be sought out
I am alone in my own home
Lonely even, at times—
For it is not in others' company that we find wholeness
It is in the company of ourselves that we find completeness
The dusty television set has not been turned on for days
The newly cleaned computer is my only solace
For it is with all of you that I share my
Deepest thoughts, my innermost words
Your faces, your pictures are reminders that I am not alone
There is an entire world of like-minded poets out there
All wishing to reach their dreams
Just as I do
The dreams of writers cannot be broken
For breaking them would break their spirits
And spirits are not meant to broken
They are to live
They are to live

My Muse

My muse is a cross between a light in the darkness
And a soul left undone—
The soul reaches to its highest levels
To where the light reaches into the darkness
Just one beam and all is transcended
In a flash—
Black letters explode across white—
Light surrounds my head and hands
As I look to my muse
To inspire
Inspire,
My muse will
Enthuse,
My muse will
Awaken
My muse will
For the light is directed implicitly to the soul
My muse is the light
My muse is the soul

When I'm Gone

When I'm gone
You're feelings might change
You'll no longer be scared like a cat when he faces a mouse
You'll no longer want to run as fast as a leopard in the wild
That's when I'm gone

When I'm gone
You might just miss me
You're heart might ache like a slow, dull heart attack
You're body might be chilled like a ten dollar martini
That's when I'm gone

When I'm gone
I will not change my mind
I will not turn my back like a quivering woman
I will not turn around to see the tears well up in your eyes
When I'm gone, it will be too late
It will be too late

The Proposal

She stood on the corner of a sidewalk in front of a Starbucks
Not wanting to turn and go, but wanting to turn and go
Two old men played dominoes at one of the coffee shop's
outdoor tables
While their dogs panted heavily in the hot Miami heat

It was Tuesday and she knew nothing of her admirer
Not knowing what the big mystery was—
Was, in itself, a charm

She had received a note, a man no less, beckoning her to the café
"Please meet me at 8:00 p.m. I'm so in love with you."
It wasn't like her to take such chances,
But the note intrigued her and she was up for a game

Her present lover, she hoped it would be
But only someone so deep in love would go through such trouble

Her chances, she took, mesmerized by the possibilities
She stayed waiting, smoking her cigarette
Until just when she had decided to leave
A man approached
He was a man of familiarity; there was no question of that
But, he approached as if he were a man unknown
He handed her red roses and kneeled down to the ground

"Marry me, love, you've waited t

The Photographer

Your passion
Your art
You capture the moment with a cunning sense—
An eye like that of black cat prowling a dark alley
Looking for every angle—
High, low, to the left, to the right, and in between
You lift up your art's tool and place it confidently to your squinted eye
You are quick and have the most exquisite instrument
An instrument even unknowing strangers to your art stop to admire
The most unique thing—
Not your tool—
Your vision
Your eyes see from a perspective no one else sees
You paint pictures with an art that doesn't use oil, acrylic, or watercolor—
Yet every picture you paint is a vision of such, but with engaging pragmatic clarity
Your pictures, your passion
Your art is my window to your world

Sexless

Menstruation comes when the Goddess of Beauty leaves
It's a terrible time
You,
Uninterested
Me,
Interested
My groin aches with pressure that you will not relieve with pleasure
It's a pressure that brings happiness and joy
The kind that makes my fierce eyes twinkle then
Stare you down like a cat sitting in the living room waiting for
Nothing

Nothing happens although penetration is all the cat wants
Penetration not from her eyes, but from
You
You selfish, desirable dog
For you are the one thing that can relieve this
Pressure

The Goddess of Beauty returns when menstruation leaves
It's a terrible time
You,
Interested
Me,
Uninterested
My heart aches to find the one true love
The one I had year's past when you looked in my eyes and saw
Love
Love is all you wanted

It’s all I wanted
So we used are arms and legs and intertwined to find
That we were compatible
Like any man and woman

And the cat stared
She stared
And she saw
Nothing

Oh, Despair!

Oh, Despair!
How my heart hangs like a teardrop from my eyes—
The teardrop hangs for you, my love—
Believe with your eyes, believe with your heart
How my heart hangs, how my teardrop hangs—
For you

Oh, Despair!
How my heart aches as if aching is essential to life—
Life cannot be without you, my love—
Believe with your eyes, believe with your heart
How my heart aches, how its life is essential—
If I am without you

Oh, Despair!
How my heart bleeds for you like an open wound left without healing—
The wound is in my heart, my love—
Believe with your eyes, believe with heart
How my heart bleeds, how my wound bleeds—
For you

Never Forget

falling out of love can be somewhat like a white aberration slowly fading away
you first fight to keep the butterflies and birds flying above your heads
you then fight to keep your identities
you, with your poetic interests and creative endeavors
the other, with their materialistic ways yet natural charms
finally, you make the decision
to never look back
but never forget
you will never forget

Christine

The sound of the train's horn
Beat through our small town
It was a wrenching noise—
One that could not be ignored
For most, it meant nothing
But for Christine, it meant everything
The ear-breaking noise that
Could shatter glass
Meant Christine's independence was over
The arrival of the train was
The arrival of her fiancé
A bold, bullheaded man
With an iron fist of frustration
Christine could not get away
From his pounding, battering words
Could not get way from his
Tearful apologies
The train and its horn—
A mere reflection of his
Pummeling insistent loud cries
And shouts
The train, as it punched its way through
Our small town
Only reminded us of Christine's plight
A plight that was like that of our own

My Voices

Voices cry out to me in soft whispers—
Like ancient ships hollowing through deep waters in moonlit nights.
They cry my name, chitter and chatter—
Sing happy songs,
And take time to gather.

The voices, I don't understand—
Never reveal their names, who or what they are…
Why they are.
Why they are here.
Why they have come.
What they have done.

My voices are me—
All one big part of me.
If I listen intently, cock my head to the side and listen and listen—
I will not hear those soft whispered voices.

No! I cannot try to hear those voices, no!
Those voices are me and I am them—
Ten solidly defined voices inside of me—
Representing me, representing them.

My Soul Knew

Before—
Long before—
My Mommy and Daddy chose to have a baby—

My Soul Knew

My Soul Knew their choice was not their own—
For it was God Who chose me for them.
It was God who made me His plan for them.
It is only God who makes these choices.

My Soul Knew

The plan God had was not only for me—
But for Mommy, Daddy, my sister, my brothers, my family, their friends—
Anyone that has ever been a part of their lives—
And anyone who is coming.

My Soul Knew

I remember the bright, sunny morning when God sat with me in a pink flower-flourished garden and tiny, baby bunnies hopping through the meadow.

"My dear little Katherine," He said. "You are very young in age, but old in wisdom. I am sending you to your Mommy and Daddy who I have specifically chosen. Your life on earth will be short, but the lesson of Faith will be long for all of those you touch."

My Soul Knew

On my short journey to do God's work I went to Mommy and Daddy—
And then I quickly left.
I fulfilled God's plan in what seemed like a lightening flash—
And I watched with Him from His Kingdom as His plan unfolded.

And My Soul Knew

Out of tragedy for Mommy and Daddy and all of those in their lives came triumph.
God's work was done by people even Mommy and Daddy didn't imagine would or even could.

God's work is still being fulfilled by Mommy and Daddy—
They pass God's Light to people just like themselves—
Offering Hope, Love, and most of all, Faith in God.

I watch Mommy and Daddy everyday with God.
God and I just nod and smile at each other because we both know I fulfilled His plan—

My Soul Knew

I look at the other babies and children in God's Kingdom—
the ones like me whom He calls His 'Special Guardian Angels'—
Probably a child of your own—
And God wants you to know—
Their Souls Knew Too

You didn't choose them—
God chose them especially for you.

We had a special purpose for you.
We had a special purpose for every person's life you touch.
We had a special purpose to foster some sort of change that is God's Will.

Our Souls Knew

Loneliness

Loneliness is a state of mind
Lost in thoughts, lost in absent words
No one but yourself to blame
It's like a bird flying in the distance
Alone and searching for its flock
Loneliness can give you the answers to questions left in your mind
It eats at you until you are blind to the outside world
Locked in aloneness, searching for companionship
Loneliness is the cure to social anxiety
It tears at your skin
And throbs deep in your core
Loneliness is something everyone must endure

I Resist

The light peeks through the red curtains of the only window in the bedroom
I squint at the florescent blue digital display of the clock on the ceiling
7 a.m.
I squint again.
Shake my head.
I had just seen the clock at 4 a.m.

The light shines brighter and time ticks on
I resist
And I resist
And I resist
Until I can resist no more

I defiantly harbor my thoughts
Try to crush them deep into my mind

Only to find that the more I crush
They're easier to find

These thoughts run through from daylight shine
'Til 4am eastern time

I resist
And resist
And wait for replies

What you send
Makes me shine

I resist
And resist

'Til I can resist no more
And crash my head to the pillow
4 am eastern time

Bridges

Water running under bridges
Keeping life at bay
Bridges lead to destiny
For this, I pray.

Being in Love

Being in love is like being home alone on a rainy day—
With your love across the seas
Sipping on a margarita.
And your heart skipping beats waiting for him to come home, to just call.

Being in love to you is conceptual.
Being in love to me is emotional.

Being
Being
Being
In love...

In love is such a combination and unification of both—
Conceptual and emotional.
For without the conceptual the emotional cannot process—
Without the emotional the conceptual cannot process.

Being
Being
Being
In love...

In love is a state of mind—
Whatever the state your mind is—
That's how in love you can be.

Without happiness within—

There is no—
Being
Being
Being
In love.

When happiness occurs within—
There is no question of—
Being
Being
Being
In love.

Agoraphobia

She weeps in a corner of her 500 square foot apartment—
Knowing nothing of what goes on the outside
People hustle by on the sidewalk and take no notice
Of apartment #602 in the lower part of the city
She cannot leave her treasured security
She cannot even motion a venture
She waits in angst for the delivery man
To bring her next meal
Paid for by her $800 Social Security check
Her grey cat lingers in the hallway
Watching her with his green eyes, a stare
It's been days since he's seen cat food and
Wonders where his next meal will come from
It's not easy being afraid of going into the world
She knows she couldn't even make it passed the door—

Chaos

The castration of this world is enough to implore insanity
Too much violence, too much danger
Too much terrorism, too many bombs

This world is filled with the evil of man
Man cannot resist urges, temptations—
Causing strife in loved ones—
The elderly and, children, no doubt

Stress is the cause of so much chaos
Chaos is the cause of the castration of the world
Too much chaos, too much stress
Hurrying here, hurrying there—
Society cannot rid itself of its strife.

Man must find a way to cleanse himself—
Lithium is not the answer
Forgetting is not the answer
Ignoring is not the answer

This depression will not cease
Until society takes a moment to stop…

Diamond Moon

Glowing diamond moon
Sends magic to the city
Sparkle white plenty

Paper Moon

Silent paper moon
Rests calmly over ocean
Seagull flies in light

Rocky Moon

Glowing rocky moon
Sheds light to earthly wonders
Giving nighttime life

Obsession

The empty page beseeches me
I wait for you
Hunger lurks in the bottom of my stomach
Red blood drops drip from the corners of my eyes
Watching the clock like some angry wildcat
My bloodshot eyes squint
The hand on the clock doesn't move
I take a drink, then another
Until the last drop of poison no longer exists
Running my hands through my hair
Scraps of strands pull out through my bony fingers
Is it too much to ask for you to be on time?
I wait for you
Like some rattlesnake watching a desert mouse
The door slowly opens and you peer through the darkened crack
Deep breath in and a grin across my face
You're here, you're finally here
The red leaves my eyes
The clock begins to tick
The glass is quickly forgotten
And I smooth my hair back into place
I walk over to you
And greet you with a delicate smile
You're home, you're finally home

The Panther and the Deer

I walk in your shadow
Only to find myself running at a constant pace
Keeping up with you is like
A black panther taking long strides
While the deer hides in the forest

I can't keep up
I can't keep up
Oh why can't I keep up?

You hold the strength and stamina and speed
That is needed to stay ahead
Like the deer
But why does the deer hide
When he has strength, stamina, and speed?
And why does the panther not keep up
When she has strength, stamina, and speed?

The panther lacks in common sense
What the deer has learned through life lessons
It's better to hide in the trees
Than to run for the rest of your life

Coming into My Own with Van Gogh

I.
St. Paul's Hospital, and I meet Vincent van Gogh.
He wants to paint a picture of me, capturing my core.
He observes me
sitting in the dingy lounge among the other patients.
I'm listening, but not talking,
Engaged, but not communicative,
There, but not really.
It's a lonely life to be a part of a group,
but have the overwhelming strength of shyness
take over.
Words live on the tongue, but are only
swallowed by fear.
Van Gogh sees this in me.
He knows
I want to belong.
I want to stand out, but I don't want to be the center.
Creativity enlightens him.
"I'll pretend I'm at the Café Terrace on the Place du Forum,"
he says,
"and I will paint you in the most magnificent scene, a place
where you can be."
He paints a view from memory
from a time when he was free from the asylum.

II.
Midnight black and blue burst from his soft-bristled paintbrush.
A scene of a bustling Paris café under a starry night emerges
from his mind onto the canvas.
A cobble-stoned street runs through the town,
and sophisticatedly clothed patrons stroll in the starlight.

He paints a figure, and then another, and another.
He dips his wand of color into the crimson oil paint
and creates an image of a woman dressed in a royal red cloak.
"This is you, amongst the others," he proclaims.
"You will stand out by color."
The woman is me and I am she,
standing out from the rest, yet
hovering in the back of the scene.

Time Holds the Wine

The heart loses itself to time
Love ferments into friend or foe
Like the vineyard grape ripens into wine
With hope and promise, love offers the sublime
Time is the measure for what the heart should know
The heart loses itself to time
The grapes wildly grow on a lush summer vine
Oh, how love also grows
The vineyard grape ripens into wine
Then comes the moment the heart must fly
Love hears nothing by an answer of "no"
The heart loses itself to time
The grapes are crushed and bottled in a line
Love doesn't bother to reason though
The vineyard grape ripens into wine
The heart waits for love in its prime
Time allows for this to be so
The heart loses itself to time
Like the vineyard grape ripens into wine

Love and Sake

Tables around her
filled with Americans eating Japanese–
A bagel roll, a shrimp tempura roll, some sake
She sat alone
a sushi bar in upper Manhattan,
drinking her own carafe.
A night time winter snow storm
fell lightly on the rushing, elbow-pushing crowd
She pondered,
where could they all being going
in such a rush?
Nothing in her life made her hurry.
Nothing made her heart beat.
Nothing made her pulse race.
The restaurant door flew open—
wind captured snowflakes blew
in, covering the floor.
Love walked in.
He unbuttoned his navy blue
pea coat, brushed off the snow from his shoulders.
His gaze fell on her, eyes opened
wide, gasping to say something.
Love looked warm and affectionate
in this cold and frigid city. No comment
on her being alone. He knew.
Love whispered in her cautious ear,
"May I join you"?
Guard let down, she welcomed his company.

He poured himself some sake.
With just one look into his accepting eyes,
the sushi-eating people, the rushing people,
all escaped her. He was the only one.
She rested her head on his shoulder,
and fell into Love.

Sushi at 9 p.m.

Our first date
I raced through the night on I-75 in my black Hyundai Accent
Hopeful with anticipation that this may be my new love
You greeted me with a grey long sleeved shirt and blue jeans
Looking unlike I imagined
Better
A kiss on the cheek and a comment
"You are hot."
I beamed because I didn't think of myself as hot
Even though I was wearing my lowest cut shirt to show off my cleavage
You pulled me into you again
Your arm around my waist and a squeeze
Your gentle, soft, lotioned hands from that point on have been my security
We walked to your grandmother's beat up Chevrolet
And you chivalrously opened the door for me
We were on our way for sushi at 9 p.m., our first meal together
The restaurant was quaint with colored paper lanterns hanging from the ceiling
You ordered a Dynamite Roll
I ordered a Bagel Roll
We ate and laughed and got to know each other
It was sushi at 9 p.m.

That Time of Year

It's that time of year
When old lives end
And new lives begin
There is a certain joy in this change
And a certain sadness that follows
Like a caterpillar metamorphosing into a red and yellow butterfly
Spreading its wings into the sky for all eyes to see
You are that butterfly
Off to new aqua and green worlds, new people, new blue skies
The learning at one level ends
And a new level of learning begins
The learning you leave is a childlike adventure
That turns to a universe of adult promise and journeys
The universe opens up to a black sky filled with brilliant white and crystal stars
Reaching beyond to infinity
And it is this time to reflect and move on
For it is this time that you begin to learn
Who you were, what you'll be, and who you'll remain
You are at a point where you come from being a boy to a man
And the pride of your family and friends for you will be felt for a lifetime
It's that time of year
Where the golden sun shines just for you
And you shine back to the world

The Seduction

With the penetration of morning sunlight
through the vertical blinds,
I open my eyes and prepare
for the sweet seduction of smoking.
It begins with the foreplay
of opening the cellophane wrapper to the cigarette box,
ripping open the aluminum foil,
and banging the box so that one cigarette stands erect.
I caress the nicotine stick between my fingers
and draw it to my mouth.
I ignite the fire to my lighter
and bring the flame to the cigarette's tip.
I suck.
The smoke enters me,
comes into the deep cavities
of my body.
I blow.
Ahhhh—
The ecstasy of inhalation, exhalation—
in, out, in, out.
It is filling.
The whole stripping process is filling—
until the last heavy outward breath,
right down to the feeling of completion
as I lay the cigarette down in its bed of ashes.
I am whole once again,
only to be seduced back to the wanting
of more orgasmic bliss
with the next cigarette.

The Epiphany

Colors surround your soul
Light shines through your spirit
Being with you is an epiphany
I cast my eyes up to you

Truth

Beyond the mist,
Hovering in the valley,
We see the truth of what is to come—
But what is truth?
But that which we see—
For truth cannot be
What we don't see

Where Do the Panthers Run?

Streams of consciousness run through cold rocks
A resting sensation in the middle of a lake
Only a mere raindrop can disturb the stillness
Even more so when the torrential storms come
Only one person can answer in truth
Only one person can listen to reason
There is no light in a cave
The darkness will take over as a mist
Surrounds the evergreen pine forest that runs parallel
To the streams of consciousness
And I ask you
Where do the panthers run
When the streams of consciousness take over the land
When country turns to city
When developers overtake the streets with strip malls
Just where do the panthers run
There's always the cave that bears no light
There's always the lake that remains still
Until the storms unsettle its rest
But where do the panthers run
When the streams of consciousness scamper

For the Sake of the Soul

Running toward an answer, a motivation, a purpose
A place where people move without thinking
Act without knowing
Race without a finish line
Too much time spent on going
Not enough time for reflecting, or loving, or nurturing
the soul—
Its energy is dried up
There is no life inside it or around it
Tired and taunted
Exhausted and exhaled
The soul does not thrive on the moving, the going, the racing
Slow down
For the sake of the soul

Lessons

With a look of youth
but a disposition grander
he labors through lessons
he can only learn
Plummeting into knowledge
Taught by seen and unseen forces
He opens his eyes to intellect
within
He opens his eyes to intellect
without
But what of these lessons
he learns?
he teaches?
Are they enough to swim through tortuous waters?
His paper of purpose
hangs on the wall
Is it enough to carry a mule's load?
Or is it too much of a load to carry?
With a look of youth
but a disposition grander
only he holds the truth
of seen and unseen lessons

Blue Bird

Blue bird chirps softly
Tenderly showing me God
Saving me with song

Detox

Rain fell quite steady
Washed the mud from my veins
Sun shines in my blood

Warmth runs through my veins
Sparkles of sunlight burst out
Filling my body

Eyes shoot light on rain
Drops turn magical colors
Forming small puddles

Songbird sings magic
Puddles expand with color
Reaching to the sky

Drops fall up to sky
Motions of colored magic
Move my arms to sky

Body filled with magic
Veins filled with sun and color
Detox rain fell steady

Mutual Adoration

Monster in a box
Your three green eyes adore me
Blue eyes adore you

Spirit Guides

Ancestors watch me
From celestial homes above
Guide my every thought

6 a.m.

Heartfelt pink sunrise
Puts glow in my empty heart
Deepest warmth inside

Dream

An angel.
A vampire.
Coming together to unite good and evil.

But what of the angel?
What of the vampire?

The angel is not so good-
The vampire, not so evil.

Together they even out
The intricacies of life
Neutralizing it
Producing a common peace of love

Together.

That is the dream—
The dream I have—
Of sweet angel and vampire kisses on October nights
Sweet kisses uniting the two—
Uniting the universe,

Uniting us.

Fire

A soul on a fire—
That's my desire.

I've longed to see your spirit ignite—
The depths of your emotions to arise—

Like the rising sun on a glorified morning day.

Fire.

Your passion is not, not there—
Just hidden below layers of fears.

I've longed to be the one to entice—
And bring them to surface like no surprise.

Fire.

You are the fire within me—
The fire I've longed to be with for the rest of my life.
Make no doubt about it, you're all I see—
I've longed for and continue to long for to be your life wife.

Fire.

You are water, I am fire—
But, deep inside you are fire
And I am water
Like an angel and a demon
We come together to balance and neutralize each other
In one heaping ball of fire.

For this heaping ball, the fire,
Is where our dreams come true.
It is within this fire
That we, and only we, have the power.

Fire.

Our complexities are many
Our intricacies are plently,
But there's no taking away, my darling—

Our fire.

God's Children Have a Purpose

All children's lives begin in God's heart—
a heart filled with warmth and love,
but also of purpose and intention.

As parents we know this.
We count on God's love for our children—
For there's no deeper love than of God's.

But when things go astray,
When our children, our babies—
Have God's purpose greater than we know—
We cannot help but question His love.

What we must realize and understand—
Is that God's purpose for our babies—
Is most certainly out of a greater love.
He loves our babies so much
That He welcomes them into his Kingdom
Before their earthly lives have a chance to begin.

No pain
No suffering
Our babies are filled with God's light and love
From the moment of conception—
To the moment God takes them to heaven.
But, why, we ask—
Why did He take my baby?
The answer, most definitely,
You will not know immediately.

But, as your life goes on without your baby—
You grieve
You cry
You question
You yearn—
And you'll soon discover
What God's intentions were for you—

You'll develop a sense of belonging.
You'll develop a stronger relationship with God.
And, finally, one special day—
You'll know your purpose in life,
The purpose God has for you.
And so, you will be complete.

Sweet Angels

Sweet snow angel—
Where do you let your wings flutter?
In a lush winter haven where red cardinals come to graze on berries
Or snow encrusted landscapes with snowflake covered pine trees?

Sweet butterfly angel—
It's springtime in the garden!
Let your wings spread out showing your rainbow of colors
And soar high to the clouds where you find life in flight!

Sweet sunflower angel—
Where does your garden grow?
With summery soft flowers and trees blowing through the warm breeze
Or a plush yard with grass ever-so-green?

Sweet pumpkin angel—
The leaves fall in your presence!
The autumn break is scented with your cinnamon stick
You are the essence of a treat or a trick!

Good Heavens, Children

Good heavens, children—
It's ten past eleven
Your sleepy heads and yawning mouths
Are well past your bedtime

What keeps you awake on this school night?
Do you need me to read you a bedtime story
To make those eyes droop to sleep time levels?

Good heavens, children—
It's time to go to bed
You need your rest for school
Paper and pens and books await you tomorrow

What keeps you awake on a school night?
Do you need me to read you a bedtime poem
To make those sleepy bodies rest at will?

Good heavens, children—
You're finally in bed
Take a rest and sleep tonight
For morning will come too soon!

Kisses

Times change and our kisses change
Passion rings in the air of our first kisses
Lips touching softly,
Then madly,
Trying to receive every essence of each other

With each kiss we feel it is our last
Two hearts beating to the rhythm of our lips
Never once missing a beat

But, just like the seasons, our kisses change
Not for the lack of love
But for the growing love we have encountered

Our lips are familiar
Comfortable
Our kisses are rich and fulfilling
To a place that only occurs with vast time
Our kisses have made us one

Monster in a Man

With a distorted smile he slivers through the island
Like a snake in the mud
Thirty two years and he still can't grasp life
The body of a man, the mind and soul of a child—
A dual persona,
A monster in the man
Abuse is the only thing he knows how to give
Words are his weapons
His tongue—a double edge sword of verbal brutality
Sadness begets anger
The lashes of his sword—
Fueled by the all too familiar hurt of a boy
The monster in the man—
A mask hiding a frail child
An unwoven ball of rage—
Covering up his inadequacy to live as a man
His only achievement in life—
Success at becoming his own worse fear—
A failure

CPSIA information can be obtained at www.ICGtesting.com
Printed in the USA
LVOW10s1329130715

446035LV00004B/185/P